CASTLE

Artist and Author:

Mark Bergin was born in Hastings, England, in 1961. He studied at Eastbourne College of Art and has specialised in historical reconstructions, aviation and maritime subjects since 1983. He has been commissioned by aerospace companies and has illustrated a number of books on flight. He has illustrated many books in the prize-winning *Inside Story* series as well as **Space Shuttle** and **Wonders of the World** in the *Fast Forward* series.

Series creator:

David Salariya was born in Dundee, Scotland, where he studied illustration and printmaking. He has illustrated a wide range of books and has created many new series of books for publishers in the UK and overseas. In 1989 he established The Salariya Book Company. He lives in Brighton, England, with his wife, the illustrator Shirley Willis, and their son.

Consultant:

Chris Gravett was born in Kent, England. He studied medieval history at the University of London and spent a number of years as a curator at the British Museum. He is currently a senior curator at the Royal Armouries in the Tower of London. He is the author of a number of books and articles on knights and castles and has acted as consultant on several others. He was involved with the film *Braveheart* and was a consultant for the BBC on their series *Ivanhoe*.

Editor:

Karen Barker Smith

Created, designed and produced by
THE SALARIYA BOOK COMPANY LTD
25 Marlborough Place,
Brighton BN1 1UB

ISBN 0 7500 2734 7

Published in 1999 by Macdonald Young Books, an imprint of Wayland Publishers Ltd, 61 Western Road, Hove BN3 1JD

You can find Macdonald Young Books on the internet at:http://www.myb.co.uk

A CIP catalogue record for this book is available from the British Library.

Repro by Modern Age

Printed in Hong Kong

CASTLE

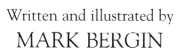

Written and illustrated by
MARK BERGIN

Created and designed by
DAVID SALARIYA

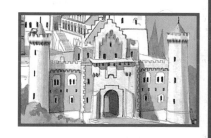

MACDONALD YOUNG BOOKS

The Age of Castles

Throughout the Middle Ages, Europe was torn apart by wars. During this period the continent was divided into many small nations. Wars between countries and feuds among barons were commonplace and were mostly attempts to plunder or take over neighbouring territories. Fortresses and castles were built for protection against enemy armies and as homes for lords and their followers. They also protected the people who worked on the castle lands and lived in the villages nearby. Between 1050-1450 castle building was at its peak – hundreds were built. From these the warrior kings and barons could command and control the surrounding lands over which they ruled. Castles were normally built on an easy site to defend, such as on a steep hillside or the top of a rocky outcrop. River crossings and alongside major road trade routes were favoured positions, making it easier to control trade and access to land. Over the centuries castles became stronger in construction to offer better protection from the weapons used against them. By the 1300s most castles could withstand almost anything other than artillery. No castle could survive a prolonged bombardment from this new invention.

Today, most castles are in ruins and are thought of as damp, cold and uninviting places to live. But, at their best, they would have been impressive sights, towering over the landscape, a physical reminder of the power and influence of the noble classes.

King

Barons

Knights

Freemen

Peasants

The nobility enjoyed a privileged lifestyle, living off the labour of the peasant classes under their control. The peasants paid taxes in the form of money or farm produce. In return, they were able to shelter within the castle walls in times of war. Barons and knights administered the law and had great power over the peasants. They acted as judges in local courts, dealing out punishments for crimes and collecting rents. More money could be raised by taxing the wind or water mills, wine presses and town shopkeepers, but such taxes were unpopular with the peasants.

The feudal system structured society in medieval times. The King was at the top and owned the majority of the land in the kingdom. He divided it among powerful barons who swore allegiance to him. These barons could not control the lands without help, so they themselves would divide it among knights. The knights had to swear loyalty to the baron and keep a number of days available to be at his service every year. The class below the knights were freemen, who were able to move from one manor to another as work was available. Finally, there were the mass of poor peasants, little more than slaves, who worked the land.

The First Castles

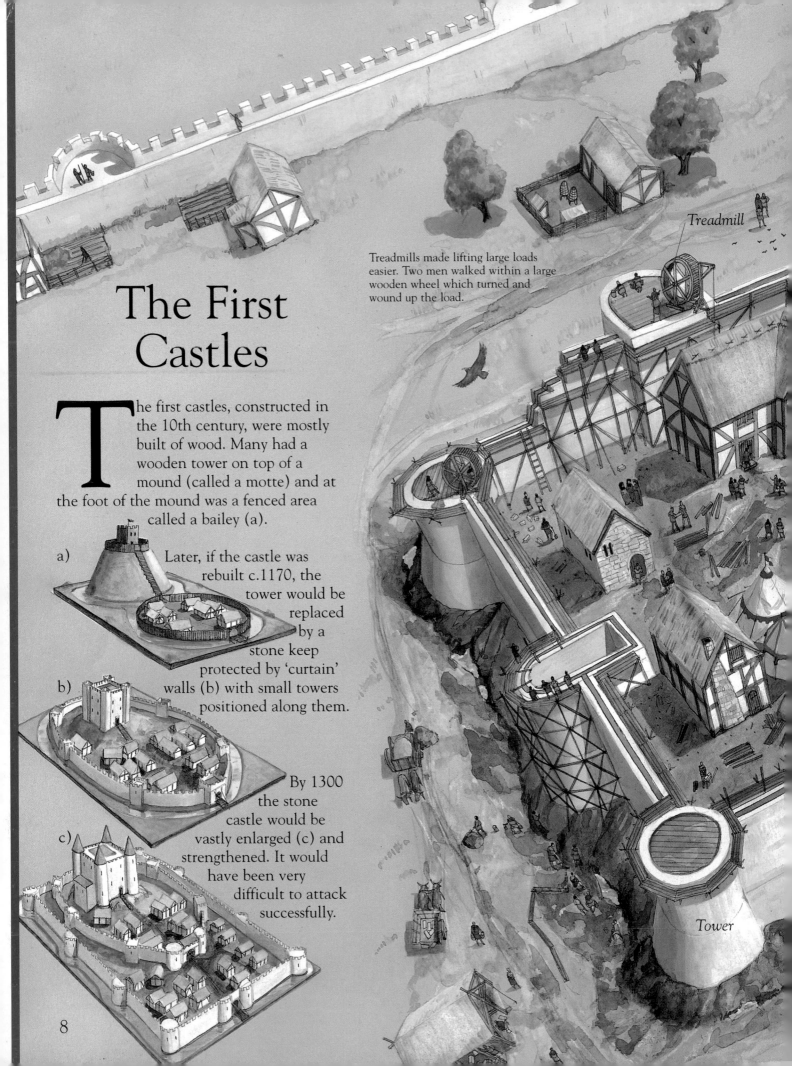

The first castles, constructed in the 10th century, were mostly built of wood. Many had a wooden tower on top of a mound (called a motte) and at the foot of the mound was a fenced area called a bailey (a).

Later, if the castle was rebuilt c.1170, the tower would be replaced by a stone keep protected by 'curtain' walls (b) with small towers positioned along them.

By 1300 the stone castle would be vastly enlarged (c) and strengthened. It would have been very difficult to attack successfully.

a)

b)

c)

Treadmills made lifting large loads easier. Two men walked within a large wooden wheel which turned and wound up the load.

Treadmill

Tower

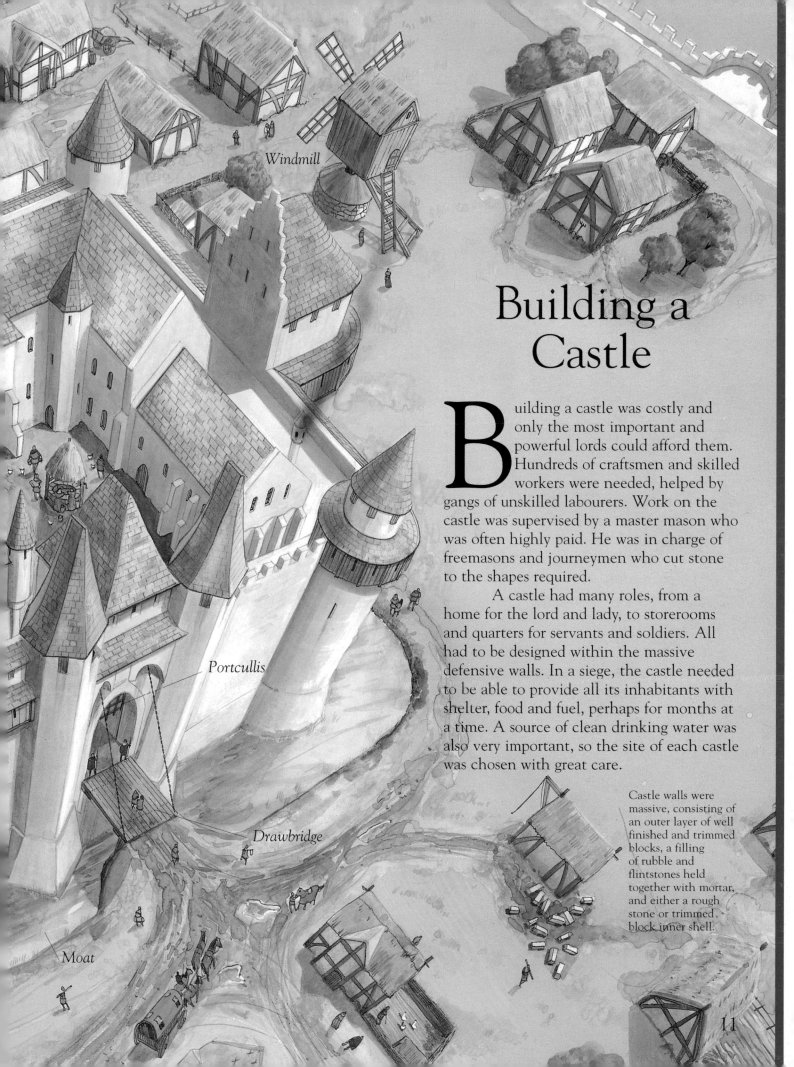

Windmill

Building a Castle

Building a castle was costly and only the most important and powerful lords could afford them. Hundreds of craftsmen and skilled workers were needed, helped by gangs of unskilled labourers. Work on the castle was supervised by a master mason who was often highly paid. He was in charge of freemasons and journeymen who cut stone to the shapes required.

A castle had many roles, from a home for the lord and lady, to storerooms and quarters for servants and soldiers. All had to be designed within the massive defensive walls. In a siege, the castle needed to be able to provide all its inhabitants with shelter, food and fuel, perhaps for months at a time. A source of clean drinking water was also very important, so the site of each castle was chosen with great care.

Castle walls were massive, consisting of an outer layer of well finished and trimmed blocks, a filling of rubble and flintstones held together with mortar, and either a rough stone or trimmed block inner shell.

Portcullis

Drawbridge

Moat

Who's Who in the Castle

A medieval baron was a formidable man. He would have been very rich, demonstrating his wealth by putting on feasts and tournaments.

A baron's wealth and influence had to be fought for and defended. Barons had to raise money through taxes and often bought the loyalty of knights and servants.

Jester
Servant
Lady's servant
Bailiff
Steward
Cook
Page
Butler
Pantler
Falconer
Knight
Reeve

Many people were needed to run a castle and serve and protect the noble landlord and lady who were the centre of castle life. A castle was like a small town, as most things anyone needed could be found within its walls, including a blacksmith, wheelwright, carpenter and candlemaker. The marshal was in charge of the garrison and often had other important duties such as deciding who should use which rooms. Clerks kept the accounts and the steward was in charge of the household. Bailiffs collected the rents and reeves managed the lord's farms. The priest held services in the castle chapel and may have acted as secretary for the castle. A pantler was responsible for buying food and provisions for the pantry. The butler dispensed the wine and the ewerer provided clean cloths to cover tables in the great hall. Pages were young boys from other noble families who came to live at the castle and helped to serve meals. Grooms worked in the stables and cared for the horses. The worst job must have been the gong farmer's, cleaning out the lavatories and moat.

The castle defences were very important and usually a number of foot-soldiers and archers were retained (or garrisoned) for defence. All these people kept the castle safe, well maintained and ensured that the noble family's lives were comfortable.

Wild animals, such as deer, wild boar, foxes, hares and rabbits provided meat for the table and larder.

Most medieval nobles enjoyed going hunting and hawking. Hunting with dogs sometimes lasted all day and was good exercise for horses and riders.

A noble woman was taught from an early age how to manage a large household. When the lord was away at court or at war she was left in charge.

The church taught nobles that they had a duty to give charity to the poor and beggars. Such money was called alms.

Baron or Lord

Lady

Marshal

Groom

Archer

The importance of archers increased in England throughout the 14th century. The government encouraged the peasantry to learn and practice the skills of archery. Good wages were paid – mounted archers could earn in two weeks what farm labourers earned in a year.

The armourer, swordsmith and arrowsmith had to make everything the soldiers would need to protect the castle or to go to war. Bodkins (arrow points), swords, axes, maces and mail shirts were all produced, although some may also have been bought in. A suit of armour was one of the most difficult items to make – it had to fit its owner incredibly well for him to be able to fight in it. They were often imported from Germany or Italy.

Large castles often had a jester. His job was to entertain the nobles and their guests with singing and story-telling. Travelling bands of jugglers, acrobats and minstrels (singers) would also be entertainment at feasts and celebrations. Lutes and bagpipes were favoured instruments.

Armourer

Juggler

Jester

Minstrels

Everyday Life

The lord and lady were the centre of castle life. They lived in grand style with lavish food, beautiful clothes and well decorated apartments. Their rooms were plastered and had colourful decorative patterns on the walls. The signs of the zodiac were among the favourite designs of the time, along with scenes from folk-tales and biblical stories. There would also have been richly embroidered wall-hangings and curtains to keep out draughts. In peace time castles were used as bases from which the nobility could govern their lands and were places of refuge away from local disease-ridden towns and villages. The lord and lady had the luxury of privacy in their castle retreat while the peasant classes usually had to cook, eat, sleep and wash in just one room.

At each corner of a square keep were towers with spiral staircases. These rose in a clockwise direction so that an attacking soldier who was climbing the stairs found it difficult to use his sword if held in his right hand. A flag or standard raised on the towers showed that the lord was at home.

The kitchen complex contained a kitchen, pantry and buttery. It was usually located away from the keep, in a separate building across the courtyard, due to the lack of space in the keep and the risk of fire. Meats such as pork and beef were roasted over a cooking fire on a spit. Other foods, such as boiled fish and vegetables were cooked in a cauldron.

Servants and peasants would eat very plain food such as soups and stews. Cabbage, leek and garlic were popular ingredients, served with rough ground brown bread.

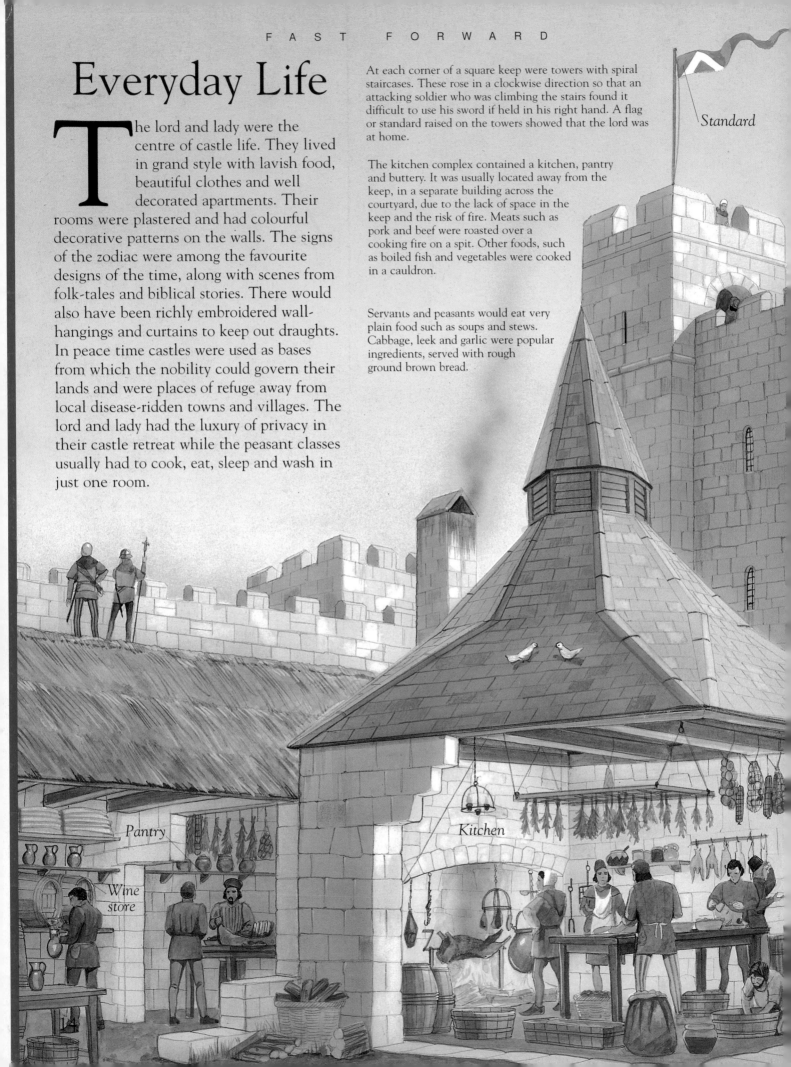

Standard

Pantry

Wine store

Kitchen

14

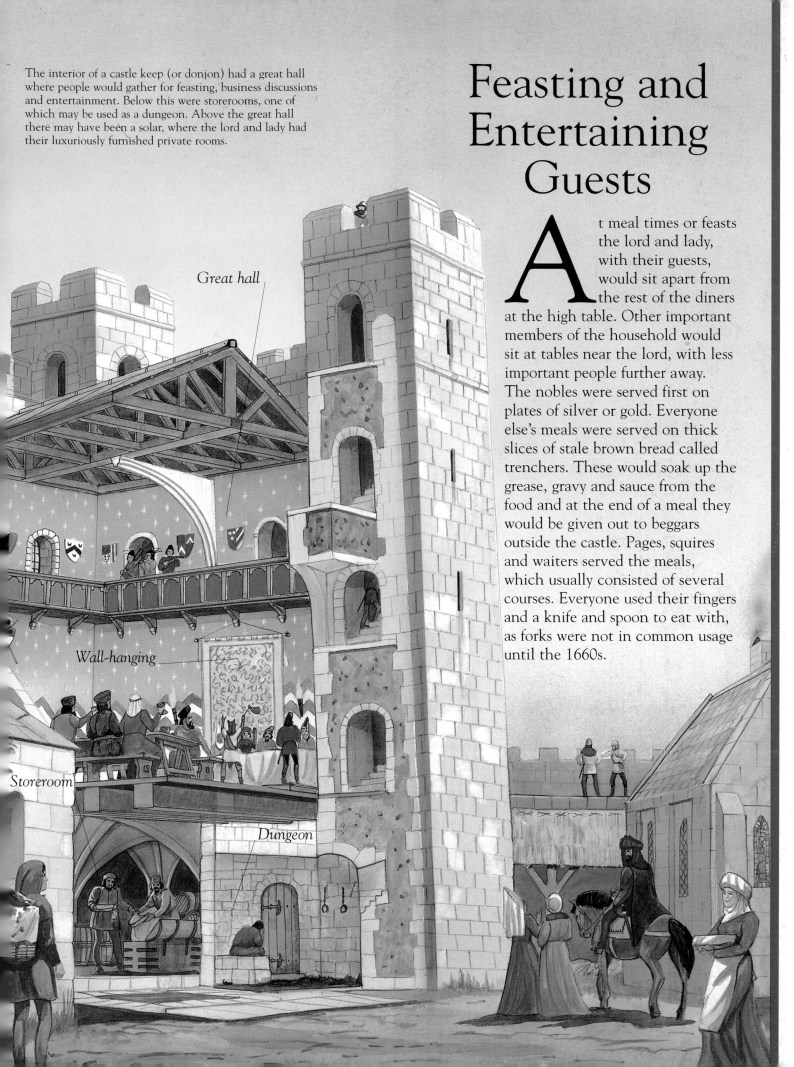

The interior of a castle keep (or donjon) had a great hall where people would gather for feasting, business discussions and entertainment. Below this were storerooms, one of which may be used as a dungeon. Above the great hall there may have been a solar, where the lord and lady had their luxuriously furnished private rooms.

Great hall

Wall-hanging

Storeroom

Dungeon

Feasting and Entertaining Guests

At meal times or feasts the lord and lady, with their guests, would sit apart from the rest of the diners at the high table. Other important members of the household would sit at tables near the lord, with less important people further away. The nobles were served first on plates of silver or gold. Everyone else's meals were served on thick slices of stale brown bread called trenchers. These would soak up the grease, gravy and sauce from the food and at the end of a meal they would be given out to beggars outside the castle. Pages, squires and waiters served the meals, which usually consisted of several courses. Everyone used their fingers and a knife and spoon to eat with, as forks were not in common usage until the 1660s.

Becoming a Knight

In his position as a page, a young boy had to wait at tables, run messages and learn all the rules of polite behaviour needed for living in noble society. French (which most people spoke anyway) and Latin were also taught. Wooden swords were used as the first weapons when learning to fight.

Page

Most young medieval boys would aspire to becoming a knight, but only those from wealthy families could be chosen to be trained as one. Learning to live as a new page, far away from family and home, must have been difficult.

To become a knight took years of training. At around the age of eight, a boy from a wealthy family would be sent to work as a page in the castle. Here he may have learned to read and write, as well as learning social skills and good manners, in the care of a schoolmaster. If the page did well and showed promise, he may have been made a squire at about the age of fourteen. He would have been assigned to a knight and accompanied him to tournaments and on war campaigns. A squire's duties also included cleaning and caring for all the knight's armour and weapons. He would learn how to dress the knight for battle, which took about fifteen minutes. During this apprenticeship the boy would also learn the skills needed to be a fighting man: horsemanship and how to handle a sword and lance in battle. A good squire could become a knight by the age of 21.

Squire

One important job for a squire was to dress his knight in plate armour (right). Most of the pieces were separate and had to be tied onto a padded cloth undertunic called an 'arming doublet'.

Plate armour

18

Lance

Quintain

Horsemanship was very important. Learning to manage a powerful stallion in combat was quite different to the cart horse a boy may have ridden before he became a squire. Handling a lance was practiced by riding at a rotating target called a quintain. If the rider was off target or too slow, the weight of the sack would hit him as it swung round.

Experienced soldiers trained young squires in battle tactics and the rules of warfare. They were shown the essential fighting skills – wrestling, how to shoot with a bow and how to use a sword, axe, lance and mace. A squire had to be fit to do all that exercise wearing plate armour, which could weigh over 30kg.

Sword

Wooden shield

At 21 a successful squire could be knighted by his lord or the knight who trained him. This dubbing ceremony often happened in church after the squire had spent the previous night alone. He was presented with his sword and spurs, and a tap on each shoulder by a sword marked his new status. Knights lived by a special code of conduct called the Code of Chivalry. They had to swear to be gentle, worthy, faithful and devoted, to defend the church and protect the poor from injustice.

Dubbing ceremony

Tournaments

Tournaments were mock battles, set up to challenge knights and entertain the noble classes. Knights gathered to display their wealth, strength and skill. Crowds would cheer for their favourites at these huge social occasions. Rewards for victory were high – the defeated may lose their valuable armour or horse to their opponent.

The prizes involved meant that tournaments were not only an opportunity for glory but also very profitable for skilled knights.

Heraldic symbols

Surcoat

Weapons and armour were specially made for tournaments. The metal tips of lances were splayed so that they would inflict less damage. Swords were blunted and maces were made of wood. Basinet helmets had bright crests on them so the knights could be identified. Shields had the top right corner removed so that a lance could be held crossed over the horse.

Shield with corner removed

Blunted sword

Lance tips

Basinet helmet

Before a tournament, large pavilions or stands were put up so the lords, ladies and judges had the best view of the action. Knights from near and far would gather in numerous tents – only the highest nobles were able to stay at the castle. The word 'joust' is believed to have come from the Latin 'juxtare' meaning to meet together.

Wargames

One of the most common forms of single combat was the tilt (or joust). The contest featured knights charging at each other with lances, on horseback. In later contests a tilt barrier was used which prevented head on collisions. It was quite common for knights to be maimed or killed in tournaments. A contest between teams of knights was known as a mêlée. There could be up to 20 on each team, all on horseback. Lances could be used but in club games the only weapons wielded were blunt swords and clubs.

Tournament games were strictly managed by judges. A knight who had cheated or dishonoured another could be forced to sit out a mêlée and so lose. Knights also fought on foot in the barriers, one on one. A fight could be stopped by heralds and men-at-arms, who would step in and force apart over-excited fighters.

Siege! Attackers and Defenders

Merlons

Machicolations

Portcullis

Until the 14th century and the invention of cannons, castles were almost impossible to destroy, so sieges were the best way to take them over. A siege was a long and serious undertaking. Whenever possible, the defenders in the castle would be persuaded to surrender, which could be done without shame or dishonour if there was little resistance shown. In this case the garrison and inhabitants of the castle would be spared. However, if the castle did not surrender its occupants might be starved into submission.

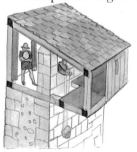

Castle defences included brattices (left). These were wooden structures which overhung the walls and had gaps in their flooring allowing quick lime, stones, pitch or boiling water to be poured over attackers. Raw animal hides or tiles may have been used to cover the brattices to protect them from fire.

Castle walls had solid pieces of masonry called merlons along the top of them, which soldiers could shelter behind. Stone machicolations were used by defenders to drop missiles on the soldiers below (right).

Merlons

Machicolations

Defenders in the castle shot arrows from narrow windows called 'arrow loops' (left). From the outside these looked like a slit in the walls but inside they were wider to allow defenders a range of angles from which to shoot. Wooden shutters hung between the merlons gave added protection to the defenders.

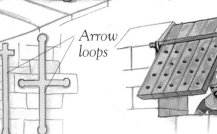

Arrow loops

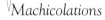

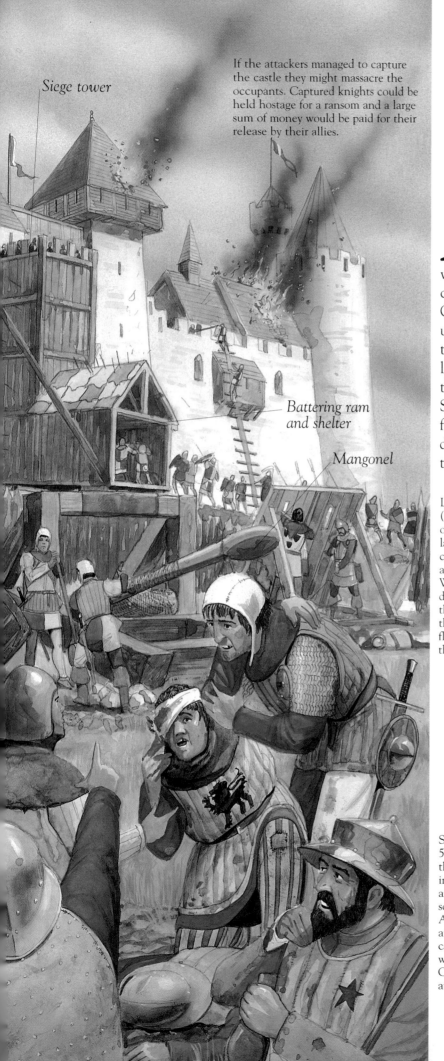

Siege tower

If the attackers managed to capture the castle they might massacre the occupants. Captured knights could be held hostage for a ransom and a large sum of money would be paid for their release by their allies.

Battering ram and shelter

Mangonel

Siege! Castle under attack

Attackers of a castle had many methods available to batter defences. Siege machines such as a mangonel or trebuchet could hurl heavy stones at weak points in the castle walls. A ballista could shoot giant javelins at defenders. One way of weakening the walls was by undermining them. A tunnel was dug under the wall with supporting beams along its length. When the beams were set on fire the tunnel collapsed, bringing the wall with it. Sieges could last for months, even years, frequently resulting in the defenders dying from starvation or surrendering to the attackers.

Large machines like the trebuchet (right) were constructed at the site of an attack. On one end of the large arm was a sling, which could contain stones, animal corpses and even severed heads. When a counterweight was dropped at the other end, the arm pivoted and the missiles were flung towards the castle.

Trebuchet

Battering ram and shelter

Siege tower

Siege towers could be between 3 and 5 storeys high, enough to look over the castle walls. They were covered in hide to protect them from fire and could be moved on wheels – some even had catapults on the top. A drawbridge could be lowered for attackers to rush across onto the castle battlements. Siege towers were successfully used in the Crusades by European knights at the siege of Jerusalem in 1099.

Castles Around the World

Around the world castles have served as fortified homes and safe bases from which to govern. Each castle reflects the society and time in which it was built. From the graceful sloping roofs of a samurai castle to the massive red stone walls of the Mogul fortress, many different architectural styles and methods can be seen. After the invention of the cannon in the 14th century, castles became of far less military importance. No castle could withstand a prolonged artillery bombardment and battles were increasingly fought by massed armies across the country, not between individual lords or barons. Society was more stable and trading became a new source of generating wealth, rather than inherited titles and fortunes.

The Romans had a very disciplined army who were able to build wooden ditch and dike forts quickly wherever they were required. These were sometimes turned into permanent stone-built army bases. This detail from a carving in Rome (above) shows a fortified building called a castrum – the origination of the word 'castle'.

The most famous castle of the Crusaders was the Krak des Chevaliers in Syria (pictured left). It was strengthened with an outer wall when captured from the Saracens.

1570 to 1690 was the golden age of Japanese castle construction. Himeji Castle (above right) was completed in 1609. This beautiful castle is covered in intricately carved and painted woodwork. It is also known as the White Egret Castle because its towers look like birds in flight. A daimyo (warlord) built the castle on such a grand scale to display the extent of his wealth and power.

28

The thirteenth century castle of Chillon (right), in Switzerland, was built on an island in Lake Geneva that had been the site of fortifications since ancient times. Its main purpose was to control shipping on the lake. Inside, the rooms were well finished and the hall was brightly decorated with painted Fleur de Lys designs.

The chateau (castle) of Usse (pictured below) is on the edge of the Forest of Chinon in the Loire valley, France. Built on the foundations of a medieval castle in 1485, the chateau is a good example of the renaissance trend towards extremely luxurious interiors and fairy tale turrets, designed to impress other nobles of the French court.

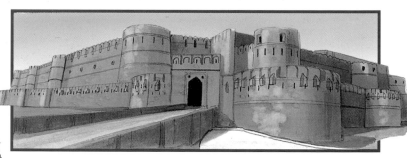

The massive fortress of Agra (above) in India has 2.4 kilometres of surrounding walls which are 21.3 metres high. Construction was started by the Mogul conqueror Akbar (1542-1605) and was finished by his grandson. The fort is three-sided and built of red sandstone.

Built for King Ludwig II of Bavaria, Neuschwanstein Castle (left) in Germany sits on a rocky outcrop high above the Lech Valley. This fantastical building was completed in 1886 at a cost of 6 million gold marks. Shortly after the castle was finished, the King drowned himself in a fit of depression.

The British royal family still uses Windsor Castle (part of which is pictured below), as a family home. In 1992 a fire destroyed several of the fine rooms, including the chapel and the banquet hall. These have been restored by a team of craftsmen and the apartments were re-opened to the public in 1998.

The noble and new merchant classes built their own structures on the sites of ruined castles and fortifications. These new buildings were not truly castles, and their merlons and machicolations served a decorative rather than defensive purpose.

Today, hundreds of thousands of tourists flock to castles around the world. Some are now just shells but many more have been preserved and cared for as national treasures. Every castle that has survived is a reminder of the people who built and lived in it.

Glossary

Arrow loops
Long narrow slits in castle walls from which arrows could be shot.

Bailey
The courtyard of a castle containing stables and other buildings.

Baron
A medieval lord in charge of large areas of land for the King.

Battlements
Stonework on the top of castle walls which protected defending soldiers.

Bodkin
An arrowhead. Usually triangular for penetrating armour.

Bombardment
A non-stop attack with cannons or catapults. A bombard was a heavy medieval cannon.

Buttery
A storeroom and dispensary for wine.

Chivalry
The knights' code of behaviour.

Crusades
The wars which started in the 11th century in the Holy Land between Christian and Muslim armies.

Curtain wall
The outer wall of a castle complex.

Drawbridge
A bridge that could be raised or moved in order to remove the crossing over a moat or ditch.

Dungeon
An underground room where prisoners were kept.

Ewerer
Servant whose duties included providing clean cloths for meal tables.

Feudal system
The organisation of the noble classes in medieval times. The King granted land to lords in return for their loyalty and provision of soldiers in wartime.

Garrison
The group of soldiers who guarded a castle.

Gatehouse
A building positioned to defend the entrance to a castle.

Heraldry
The system of symbols and colours identifying noble families.

Holy Land
The region made up of Israel, Jordan and Syria.

Jousting
A tournament game in which two knights on horseback charged at each other holding lances. The aim was to knock the opponent off their horse. Also known as the tilt.

Keep
The central tower in a castle where the lord and his family's apartments were. Also known as a donjon.

Lance
A long painted spear used by a knight on horseback.

Longbow
A wooden bow made from yew. They were often as tall as a man and were a favourite weapon of the English.

Machicolations
Stonework overhanging the castle walls from which objects could be dropped on attackers.

Mangonel
A very large catapult used as a siege weapon.

Merlons
The solid parts between the gaps on the top of the battlements.

Moat
A deep water-filled ditch around a castle. An important part of a castle's defences.

Motte
A mound of earth on top of which a wooden tower would be built.

Plate armour
Armour made up of body hugging sheets of metal.

Portcullis
A gridded gate made of wood covered in metal that could be raised and lowered at the entrance to a castle.

Quick lime
Powder which burned skin and clothing on contact.

Quintain
An apparatus for training to joust with a lance.

Ransom
A sum of money demanded for the release of a captive.

Siege
Surrounding a castle and cutting off all supplies to it in order to force its defenders to surrender.

Solar
A private sitting room for the lord and lady in a castle.

Squire
Apprentice and personal servant to a knight.

Standard
A flag showing symbols or devices which identifies a lord, king or other member of noble society.

Tournament
A festival consisting of mock battles between knights.

Trebuchet
A giant catapult apparatus used in sieges.

Castle Facts

The castle at Herstmonceux in Sussex, England, is a large rectangular building of red brick. It has a moat and high walls but its main defences are the towers behind the drawbridge. These were equipped with artillery and had fighting platforms on the top.

In the 13th century, Catalan kings rebuilt the 8th century Arab fortress the Alcazer (below) in Segoria, Spain. The site makes good use of a natural rocky outcrop. The castle was destroyed by fire in 1862 and has since been totally restored.

Castle Hedingham, built in 1215 in eastern England, is a typical example of a square stone keep. A turret guards and strengthens each corner.

King Edward I besieged Kenilworth Castle, England in 1266. The castle did not succumb to the king's attack for a year because it had such impressive defences. Its water defences made undermining impossible and it could only be bombarded by the largest long range machines.

Beaumaris Castle in Wales was designed with two curtain walls, one inside the other, each fortified with towers. King Edward I began construction in 1277, but he died before it was completed and building work stopped in 1307.

The Pfalzrafenstein (below) is unusual for its hexagonal shape. It was built by Ludwig of Bavaria as a toll station in 1327 and stands on a natural island near Kaub in the Rhine River. Later additions to the roofs were made in the 17th century.

Shrewsbury Castle in England originally had a wooden tower built on the motte. However, in 1270 it collapsed of old age.

The Krak des Chevaliers (Castle of Knights) in Syria was taken over by French crusaders in 1099. They rebuilt it to be well fortified and to house a large garrison. It had its own aqueduct and reservoir to provide water for its inhabitants.

The stronghold of Dornie Castle (above) stands isolated in the highlands of Scotland. It is a fine example of a fortified tower house with water on all sides making it easy to defend. It is linked to the mainland by a small bridge.

Neuschwanstein Castle in Germany was extremely luxurious. It had a central heating system installed and the kitchen even had hot and cold running water. The features that were copied from original medieval castles, like the battlements, are purely decorative and serve no defence purpose at all.

Construction of Borthwick Castle near Edinburgh, in Scotland, began in 1430. Its design is simple but very strong. Over 13,000 tonnes of stone were used for the outer facing and the walls are over 4 metres thick.

Himeji Castle in Japan has a complex system of defences. The network of courtyards is protected by stone walls and 20 gatehouses, inside which the 8 storey main keep is linked to 3 smaller keeps. Although the ramparts and courtyard walls were made of stone, the majority of the castle itself is made of timber.

The Eagle Tower of Caernarvon Castle in Wales is over 35 metres high. It once had its own water-gate and dock which could have been an escape route to the sea as well as allowing supplies in if under siege.

The Palace of the Popes is in Avignon, France. It was built in 1370, at a time when there were two rival popes.

Index

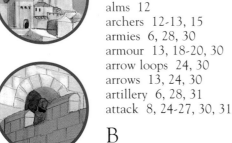